Practical Foundations for Independent Learning

SALLY FEATHERSTONE
with
ROS BAYLEY

We Can Do It!
Practical Foundations for Independent Learning

ISBN 1 904187 79 X

Text by Sally Featherstone and Ros Bayley
Designed and illustrated by Kerry Ingham
Additional editing by Phill Featherstone

©Featherstone Education, 2004
All rights reserved
Text © Sally Featherstone & Ros Bayley, 2004
Illustrations © Kerry Ingham, 2004

The right of Sally Featherstone and Ros Bayley to be identified as the authors of this work has been asserted in accordance with Sections 77 and 78 of the Copyright, Designs and Patents Act, 1988.
All rights reserved. This book is sold subject to the condition that it shall not, by way of trade or otherwise, be sold, lent, hired out or otherwise circulated in any form of binding or cover other than that in which it is published and without a similar condition, including this condition, being imposed upon the subsequent purchaser. No part of this publication may be reproduced or transmitted in any form or by any means, electronic or mechanical, including photocopying, recording or duplication, or stored in any information storage and retrieval system, including the internet, without the prior written consent of the publisher.

First published in the United Kingdom in 2004 by
Featherstone Education Ltd
44-46 High Street, Husbands Bosworth, Lutterworth LE17 6LP, United Kingdom
www.featherstone.uk.com

Introduction	page 2
Construction	page 4
Creative Development	page 10
Messy Activities	page 16
Sound and Movement	page 22
Outdoor Play	page 28
Role Play	page 34
Stories	page 40
Writing	page 46
Systems, Structures and Organisation	page 52
Further Reading	page 56

Introduction

This book is about empowering children. It is about giving them the environment and experiences which will equip them to become willing and motivated learners. It is about enabling them to engage in the processes of their own learning and begin to take responsibility for it

There are factors which work against independence in most settings. Any organisation needs systems, processes, rules which make for smooth and safe running. They are part of an orderly society. But, however sensitively implemented, some of them will inevitably limit the scope of the individual to do exactly as he or she likes. It is very easy to use conditions imposed on us, or rules we have created, as reasons for not giving children the freedom to decide and act. So throw out the rule book! Or at least take another look at it and ask how much of it is necessary, and whether anything there might be inhibiting children's independence.

Developing independence requires time. Choosing, experimenting, exploring options, thinking and talking about possibilities all need time and space to develop. It is easy to become impatient when children are involved and time is short. Sometimes it seems as though they are being deliberately slow, and perhaps sometimes they are, although in our experience this is rare. Under pressure to get things done, to beat the clock and to meet our (sometimes self-imposed) schedules it is tempting to do things ourselves and not wait for the children. However, we should never forget that time is a vital learning resource, and we need to ensure that children have plenty of it.

Foundations for Independence, which this book complements, includes guidance on the physical setting, space and access. Accommodation varies from one setting to another, and some voluntary and independent providers have to endure particularly difficult conditions. In some schools Nursery and Reception classes are banished to the least attractive and most inconvenient spaces. And of course, all settings are short of money. However, we should not use inadequacies in the environment and resources to justify not doing what we know we should. With imagination, problems can often be turned into opportunities. And even when they can't, there is much that can be done within even the most basic setting to help children become independent learners.

Some practitioners are worried about the consequences of encouraging children to be independent. 'Will independence mean constant confrontation and conflict?', 'How can I be sure children won't take inappropriate risks?', 'Will independence be a threat to my position as an adult?', 'What about my need to be needed?'. These are all natural and fair questions. This book provides help and reassurance in dealing with these issues.

We Can Do It!

The first step is to identify the things in the setting which inhibit loosening the reins, surrendering some control, being willing to adapt or abandon careful plans and allow the children to take the lead in deciding where the curriculum should go. Sometimes it may be necessary to persuade colleagues of the value of a different approach, changing not just minds but hearts, because this is the way to change practice.

Judy Miller in her book 'Never too Young' provides a useful list of what children need to become independent learners:

- **opportunity** – to try things for themselves.
- **experience** – of practising independence from an early age.
- **role models** – of adults and other children. What we do has far more influence than what we say.
- **expectations** – that they can and will become independent learners, given time and opportunity.
- **motivation** – created by rewarding and praising effort and success.
- **information** – to empower them to make choices and decisions.

With this list in mind, 'We Can Do It' explores some of the key aspects of learning:

- **Imaginative and Role play**
- **Outdoor play**
- **Construction** (large and small)
- **Stories, puppets and plays**
- **Writing**
- **Computers and other ICT**
- **Creative activities** (paint, modelling, collage)
- **Messy activities** (sand, water, dough, malleable materials, wood)
- **Cooking**
- **Sound, music and dance**

The aim is that by giving special attention to these areas, practitioners will help the children in their care to become more independent in their learning and in their lives.

There is an ICT 'box' in each chapter which emphasises how ICT can be used most effectively as a resource for other areas of learning, rather than being explored as a topic in itself. Similarly, each chapter provides plenty of opportunities for number activities – weighing, counting, estimating, sharing – and so there is not a separate chapter on maths or number. Specific number activities can be found in 'The Little Book of Maths Activities' and 'The Little Book of Maths Songs & Games', both published by Featherstone Education.

There are ways to develop independence and autonomy in every setting, throughout the day in all activities; they are part of the ethos of the setting and need consideration when planning the Foundation Curriculum. This book takes a selection of aspects and explores how they can be used to help children to become more independent. They are not the whole story, but we hope they will provide ideas, perhaps inspiration, and above all the desire to help children to feel and say, 'We Can Do It!'

Construction

 ## Introduction

> "One of the areas in which three and four year old children make the most progress concerns the development of fine motor control. This can be defined as the ability to co-ordinate the action of the eyes and hands together in performing skilful adaptive movements."
>
> Audrey Curtis in 'A Curriculum for the Pre-School Child'.

Construction is an important way in which children practise and perfect fine motor control. Without good hand-eye co-ordination reading and writing become very difficult. The construction area is where real learning and language development often take place, and so should be a regular focus for observation by adults. Construction activities contribute to all areas of learning. Their relevance can be seen in the collaborative aspects of personal development, in shape and space in maths, in science, technology, physical skills and creativity.

 ## Links with Early Learning Goals

Personal, Social and Emotional Development

- Maintain attention and concentration.
- Work as part of a group or class, taking turns and sharing fairly, understanding that there need to be agreed values and codes of behaviour for groups of people, including adults and children, to work together harmoniously.

Language, Communication and Literacy

- Use language to imagine and recreate roles and experiences.

Mathematics

- Use language such as more, less, greater, smaller, heavier, lighter to compare two numbers or quantities.
- Talk about, recognise and recreate simple patterns.
- Use language such as circle, or bigger to describe the shape and size of solids and flat shapes.
- Use everyday words to describe position.

Knowledge and Understanding of the World

- Investigate objects and materials by using all of their senses as appropriate.
- Build and construct with a wide range of objects, selecting appropriate resources, and adapting their work where necessary.
- Select tools and techniques to shape, assemble and join the materials they are using.

Physical Development

- Move with confidence, imagination, in safety and with control and co-ordination.
- Use a range of small and large equipment.
- Handle tools, objects, construction and malleable materials safely and with increasing control.

Creative Development

- Express and communicate their ideas, thoughts and feelings by using a widening range of materials, suitable tools, imaginative and role play, movement, designing and making, and a variety of songs and instruments.

Explanation/discussion

Most children enjoy making things, but boys and girls approach construction in different ways. Research into brain development tells us that boys and girls develop different parts of their brains at different ages. From the beginning of nursery, boys will opt for practical activities and will choose frequent change. Girls will choose books, painting and drawing, and will spend twice as long on an activity as boys. This is because the left side of the brain (the side linked to analytical skills and language learning) develops earlier in girls than in boys. By providing a wide range of construction activities we help boys and girls to develop both sides of their brains. For girls, construction gives opportunities to work in three dimensions, in patterns and shapes with mathematical connections, right brain activities. It gives boys the chance to concentrate and to improve those essential skills which come from the left brain.

Building with three-dimensional objects falls into three main areas:

Bricks — using bricks of various sizes and in various materials

Joining sets — using joining sets such as Lego, Sticklebricks, Mobilo

Recycled & found — using recycled and found materials, such as cartons, card tubes, reels, spools, plastic containers and bottles, tops, string, wool, fabric, plastic, paper and card.

While recognising these three main areas, we should support children who want to combine elements from two or more areas. Small world people make a contribution to brick play, found materials can enhance joining sets, and access to card, pens, reference books and pictures should be made as easy and inviting as possible.

Simply including small world people can be enough to stimulate girls' interest, while access to books and mark making equipment will extend the initial construction phase for many boys. Foster attitudes where children go readily to each other and to adults for help, and can experiment without fear of failure.

Space is vital for constructions of all sorts. Brick play needs a flat, soft surface inside or out. A large piece of carpet is ideal. Children often prefer to work with construction and found materials on tables or benches, and these areas can include a shelf for storing unfinished and completed models and structures.

Time is all-important in planning construction activities. Children need that 'time for sustained concentration' which gives them room to develop the play, process it in their minds and return to it later or even the next day. Children have not necessarily finished an activity just because we say it is time to pack away!

Case Study – Construction

The room is set up with clearly defined areas for different activities. Four children (three boys and a girl) are playing on a carpeted area with a large set of small wooden bricks. They have made a huge layout of the bricks in a complicated design of roads, buildings, trees, parks and fields. As they work, individuals fetch additional resources – a basket of farm animals, a village set, some cars and people. Other children come to watch the construction as it grows. They contribute ideas and some get involved in the play. The teacher observes as the scene develops. She says nothing, but makes a few notes and takes a series of photos as the construction grows over several days with different children involved. At group times she encourages the children to talk about what they are doing, modelling language and vocabulary. She suggests books and stories that might be of interest.

One day she offers a set of road signs. This sparks new enthusiasm, and a flurry of writing follows. Children make signs and notices, including one saying 'plese kep off'. They choose small sticks, plastic bottle tops and pieces of card from the carefully organised boxes of materials, each labelled with its contents, to make more signs for the construction. They give it a name: 'Brikland'. Martha fetches a peaked cap and a shoulder bag from the prop box. She has been to a model village and knows about tickets. She makes some from paper, decorates each one and stands by a notice, which says 'brikland pay here'.

The teacher provides a box of money and the play develops into the next phase. Construction has now overlapped into role play. Eventually the work on the village expands into all areas of the curriculum, providing opportunities in maths, language, science, technology, for visits and walks in the locality and for the development of fine motor skills. The extended building and reorganisation of the construction involves plenty of practice in negotiation and compromise.

Case Study CONCLUSION

In this example of **construction** the children have plenty of opportunities to control and shape the activities, and this leads to a range of valuable experiences which the practitioner had not planned. Note how she acts as a resource, providing just the right amount of stimulation and encouragement to keep things moving forward.

Quality Checklist ✓

Ask yourself –

- Do we give this area of the curriculum the status it deserves? Do we observe and document what the children do, and feed back what we see by sharing photos and writing down their words? This raises self-esteem and self-image, and gives the activity status with others.
- Are the resources for all sorts of construction well organised, attractive, well maintained, high quality and in sufficient supply? Do they stimulate and sustain interest and involvement?
- Do we encourage children to mix and combine construction materials?
- Do we take time and care when organising found and recycled materials for children?
- Are children encouraged to develop the play? Are we able to leave unfinished or ongoing constructions overnight or over longer periods? If not, what can we do about it?
- Do children feel comfortable combining sets of equipment to extend their play?
- Can children move from area to area, following their needs to make marks, integrate other materials, revisit activities, refer to books during their play?
- Do we discuss projects with the children, helping them to make links in their learning through discussion and sensitive suggestions? Do we consult them when buying or collecting new items for construction?
- Are difficulties and obstacles discussed and solutions tried?

When children are making more permanent constructions:

- do they have the tools, materials and support to ensure successful outcomes?
- does the glue really stick?
- are the scissors sharp enough?
- will the paint cover the surfaces?
- are difficulties and obstacles discussed and solutions tried?

We Can Do It

Resources for construction

It will help to avoid conflict if you can make sure that there is plenty of everything to go round. Either that, or work with the children on devising and developing turns and routines which will give everyone a fair chance to play.

Some resources for construction need regular maintenance

- Wooden blocks should be splinter free, stable, and well organised for access and storage.
- Plastic and foam bricks should be cleaned regularly and stored in lightweight bags or crates so that children can carry them easily.
- Make sure glue, staplers, tape and so on are available and easy to use.
- Display children's own plans and drawings of their constructions.
- Make sure construction sets have a good mixture of standard parts and additions such as wheels, roof tiles, arches, cogs, figures.
- Store sets in several smaller containers so children can get them out independently and work in smaller groups or different locations.
- Give opportunities to mix and combine different sets for bigger, more complex projects.
- Add books, displays of photos, posters and pictures to expand children's ideas and thinking.
- Make a space for keeping unfinished and finished models and structures.

ICT Box

- Offer children calculators, stopwatches, 'phones and so on to use when they are working. As they use them in roleplay, they will be getting used to the feel and the position of the keys.
- Offer the ideas and the materials to make working or replica dashboards and control panels.
- Show children how to make simple circuits with bulbs and batteries, so they can make their own switches, lights and buzzers for their models
- Use and talk about remote control toys and vehicles. Offer old remotes for use in roleplay.
- Look for simple computer construction programmes.

We Can Do It!

Getting Started with construction!

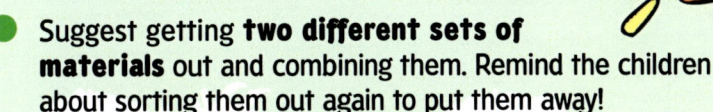

- **Talk** about construction, encourage children to plan where they will start and what they might make.
- Use **pictures, stories, objects** and characters as inspiration for brick play.
- Suggest getting **two different sets of materials** out and combining them. Remind the children about sorting them out again to put them away!

- **Collect a small basket** of assorted construction parts, and talk about what they might represent.
- Ask the children to bring in some **found materials** from home and spend time as a group sorting and discussing them, organising them and making temporary constructions. Take time over several days to get to know the materials and their properties before incorporating them in some more permanent constructions.
- **Mix up resources**. Add chalk to the box of cars. Put a small basket of mark makers and cards in the Lego box. Add cars and people to brick baskets.
- Try some **space people** figures.
- Use **big bricks** to make houses, shops, boats for role play.

- Suggest **group play or timed sessions** working on the same construction and see what develops.
- Sometimes have a week with **no glue** in the construction area. Or a week with **no scissors**. These challenges will test ingenuity.

- Make a **collection** of found materials. Leave it out and see what happens.
- Cut out some **card circles** for wheels and provide split pins. Ask the children how they could use them.
- Construction is about **solving problems**. Look at some of the problems in your setting and ask the children how they could be solved.

Try these themes as starters...

- Visit a building site, take some photos.
- Put a new 'found' resource in the area: film containers, garden sticks, reflective tape.
- Give them a real problem to solve – fixing, lifting, making or mending something.
- Take large 'found' materials outside (guttering, big boxes, tubes from rolls of carpet and so on).

Creative Development

> "Creativity is not simply a matter of letting go. Serious creative achievement relies on knowledge, control of materials and command of ideas. Creative education involves a balance between teaching knowledge and skills, and encouraging innovation."
>
> DfEE, All Our Futures: Creativity, Culture and Education

 ## Introduction

Creative development has huge benefits for self-esteem and achievement. Observation and research confirm the impact of creative development on motivation and success in learning, and it is essential for everyone in the team to do everything possible to help children discover their creativity. "Creativity depends on the ability to see things in fresh ways. It involves learning from past experiences and relating this learning to new situations, as well as thinking along unorthodox lines and breaking barriers." Bernadette Duffy, 'Supporting Creativity and Imagination in the Early Years'.

Children need help in developing attitudes which support their creative ideas and impulses, and the persistence to keep going when things don't work out straight away. Practitioners also need to understand and accept that creativity can be a messy process.

Links with Early Learning Goals

Language, Communication and Literacy
- Use language to imagine and recreate roles and experiences.

Knowledge and Understanding of the World
- Investigate objects and materials by using all of their senses as appropriate.
- Select appropriate resources, adapting their work where necessary.
- Select tools and techniques to shape, assemble and join the materials they are using.

Physical Development
- Use a range of small and large equipment.
- Handle tools, objects, construction and malleable materials safely and with increasing control.

Creative Development
- Express and communicate their ideas, thoughts and feelings by using a widening range of materials, suitable tools, imaginative and role play, movement, designing and making, and a variety of songs and instruments.
- Respond in a variety of ways to what they see, hear, smell, touch, feel.
- Explore colour, texture, shape, form and space in two and three dimensions.

 ## Explanation/discussion

Supporting the independent creative development of children is one of the most skilled and subtle aspects of the work of early years practitioners and the younger the children, the more help will be needed, and the more sensitive it needs to be!

We Can Do It!

Adults can help by:

- Demonstrating new materials, equipment and techniques and by drawing, painting and making models alongside the children.
- Supporting children in taking risks and experimenting, and by making sure that there are opportunities for children to co-operate and collaborate on projects.
- Introducing them to art from cultures other than their own, and from local and national artists; this will broaden children's minds and stimulate their imaginations.
- Openly valuing children's creative expressions, especially when they are being displayed or discussed.

Help every child to have ownership of their creative work

- Show them what the materials will do and then stand back and allow them to use them in their own way.
- Be flexible; be prepared to rearrange activities so children can continue to work on something they are involved in.
- Respect their ideas, even when they conflict with what you would most like - the child who paints a picture and then wants to cover the whole thing with black paint may really need to do this!
- Involve them in setting up the creative area. Ask questions like 'What would you like to work with today?'. Let the children cover the surfaces, get the equipment ready, mix the paint, put out collage materials and so on.

If possible, let children decide **where** they would like to draw, paint or model. Painting outside will provide a very different experience from painting inside and will spark different ideas.

Provide spaces where children can work. Ask them where and how they would most like to display their work. **Involve** them in selecting and ordering resources and equipment for the creative area.

Show children how to use a camera so that they can record the progress of their projects. Above all ensure that children feel able to experiment, take risks and attempt to express their thoughts and feelings.

We Can Do It!

Case Study – Creative Development

Jessie had been fascinated when Adina, her keyworker, had taken in some of her own artwork to share with the children. Adina liked to paint with watercolours, and had shown the children how she worked. The group enjoyed looking at her paintbox and brushes, and spent a long time talking about all the different colours. Jessie was particularly fascinated by the picture of Adina's garden. She asked Adina countless questions about what was in her garden and the way she had painted it.

The following day, as she arrived at her setting, Jessie announced she was going to make a picture of her garden. Adina found some block colours and showed Jessie how to mix water with the colour.

Jessie chose some paper and set to work, becoming so engrossed in exploring the effects of the paint that she almost forgot that she had intended to paint her garden. Adina watched and asked her about the things that were in her garden.

"I want to do my swing and my slide, and the tree, and all the flowers," said Jessie. "We've got lots and lots of flowers."

Jessie was now interested in the bold lines of her swing and her slide, which she painted with great deliberation. She began to look for some green paint, and realising that there was none she carefully spooned some green powder paint into a pot, added water and mixed until the paint was the colour and texture she needed.

Her next step was to make the flowers. She collected some art straws and shiny coloured paper. Laying these beside her painting she fetched scissors to cut up the paper and art straws to make flowers. She placed the finished flowers on top of the painting, expecting them to stick to the paint. Jessie began to carry her finished piece of work to the drying rack.

"Oh no!" she cried, as all her carefully cut flowers fell to the floor.

Adina intervened to offer support and together they picked up the pieces.

"How do you think we could stop all your flowers falling off?" prompted Adina.

"I think I need to glue them," said Jessie.

"You go and get the glue then," suggested Adina, "and I'll finish picking up your flowers."

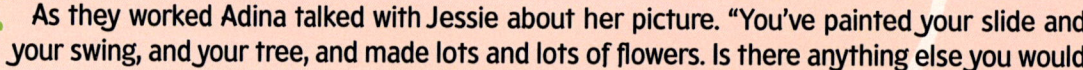

As they worked Adina talked with Jessie about her picture. "You've painted your slide and your swing, and your tree, and made lots and lots of flowers. Is there anything else you would like in your picture? You could paint yourself and your friends playing in the garden."

"No," said Jessie. "I like my picture. I like my picture!"

"So do I!" said Adina. They worked on in silence until all the flowers were stuck.

"There," said Jessie, "now I can put it to dry. They are all stuck."

With great satisfaction Jessie took her completed picture to dry.

Jessie knew what she wanted to do and was clearly in control of the creative process. She called on Adina when she needed technical help.

Case Study CONCLUSION

In this example of **creative development**, Adina provided examples and demonstration of her own adult creativity. She introduced new materials, then stepped back, allowing the children to explore the new materials and techniques, adding them to their repertoire. Demonstration of new techniques and resources is important. How children then use these new stimuli and combine them with others should be left to them. Do you introduce and demonstrate new techniques, materials and equipment? Do you encourage each other to share hobbies and creative interests with the children?

Quality Checklist

Ask yourself –

- Do we, as a team, know enough about the ways in which children develop creativity?
- How do we plan for children's creative experiences? Do our plans focus on outcomes or processes?
- How sensitive are team members when they interact with children in the creative area? Do we 'tune-in' to what they want to explore, listen carefully to ascertain their purpose and support them in achieving their goals, even when they are different from ours?
- Have we worked with parents and carers to help them understand the importance of process over outcome?
- Could we involve the children more in decisions about which materials they would like to use and the ways they would like to use them?
- Do we display children's work in ways that really respect their representations, or do we try to 'pretty' them up in the interests of a 'better display'?
- Do the children have independent access to a wide range of resources and media?
- Does everyone in the team support creativity in all areas of the work of our setting, or is it something left to a few who are considered the 'artists' in the group?
- Do we share our own creative interests with the children – flower arranging, gardening, cake decorating, home improvement, sewing, as well as painting and drawing?

Resources for creative development

A well-resourced creative area is a challenging and exciting place for independent learners. Ideally, it is situated near a water supply with a suitable floor surface and space for several children to work. Children should be able to choose to work at a table or an easel, to work outside or inside.

Your creative area may have

- Boards fixed to walls and outdoor easels.

- Opportunities to investigate a wide range of materials – textiles, clay, dough, wool, printing - accessible and stored at child height.

- A range of paper in various weights, colours and sizes, paint. A range of brushes for different purposes and a collection of utensils for applying paint – palette knives, brooms with soft bristles, sponges, sprays, old washing-up liquid containers. Date stamps and name stickers so children can label their own work.

- Space for completed work to dry and for projects to be left out for completion later.

- Aprons, dustpans and brooms which are accessible so that the children can be encouraged to take responsibility for themselves and their surroundings.

- The work of famous artists displayed and discussed. The book corner or library should contain books about famous artists and borrowed objects from a local museum. Encourage the children to talk about what they like and why.

- Information about local galleries where children and parents are welcomed by staff!

- Displays used as starting points for talking about different media and the different ways in which the artists have worked.

ICT Box

- Use painting and drawing programmes which encourage creativity, not just colouring in.
- Help children to learn how to scan, cut and paste, repeat and save their work.
- Let children use the photocopier sometimes to copy their work to save or give to others.
- Use light boxes and OHP machines to project objects and make colour creations with transparent materials.

We Can Do It!

Getting creative!

- Talk about creative work, and encourage children to plan, explain and discuss what they are doing. Put together interesting things for them to observe, draw and paint.

- Spend time observing the creative area, it is often an area neglected by adults. Let children see you are interested in what they are doing. Photograph their projects at various stages of development so they can display the photographs. Help them to recall and discuss the process.

- Try not to have preconceived ideas about what children will do and how they will represent their view of the world. Don't let your voice, body language or expression affect how children feel about their work.

- Ask open-ended questions that encourage children to see things in fresh ways such as; What are some of the things we could do with these materials? I wonder what would happen if ...? How else could you use this...?

- Support children in linking experiences by asking questions such as; Do you remember what happened when we added glue to the paint? Can you remember another way to...?

- Allow children to make mistakes, for example when you see them trying to join two things together in a way you know will not work, don't do it for them – let them experience failure, support them through it and encourage them to learn from the experience and start again.

- Share your own creative experiences with them – if you paint, draw, sew, sculpt, collect shells, grow flowers, bring your creativity into your setting.

- Make time to express your creativity – it takes creative adults to nurture creativity in children.

Try these ideas as starters...

- Display a vase of twigs, or flowers or a collection of seeds or leaves.
- Collect a scrapbook of faces cut from magazines.
- Use sticks, feathers, straws for painting instead of brushes.
- Add a bowl of coloured feathers, smooth pebbles, sequins or coloured aquarium gravel to the creative resources.
- Paint with mud, clay, food colouring.

Messy Activities

"Children need to work with a range of materials ... for example, wet and dry sand, coloured and clear liquids, compost, gravel and clay."

DfEE, All Our Futures: Creativity, Culture and Education

Introduction

'Messy' activities are an essential part of work in all early years settings. When playing with sand, water, malleable materials and wood, children can learn skills, concepts, attitudes and approaches that are transferable to every area of learning. In a well-planned setting they can do this in a way that supports the development of independence and initiative. But this does not simply happen; it requires that the staff team give time and energy to ensuring that such opportunities are there, and the range of opportunities in messy play is only limited by our imagination. Some of the most exciting play with sand, water, malleable materials and wood happens when practitioners use their creative impulses and introduce unusual materials into the area. Once children have seen the new possibilities these offer, their imaginations are fired and they can go on to use these materials in their own way.

Links with Early Learning Goals

These aspects of your provision will facilitate development across every area of learning but some of the major goals are:

Language, Communication and Literacy
- Use language to imagine and recreate roles and experiences.

Knowledge and Understanding of the World
- Investigate objects and materials by using all of their senses as appropriate.
- Find out about, and identify, some features of objects and events they observe.
- Select tools and techniques they need to shape, assemble and join the materials they are using.
- Select appropriate resources, and adapt their work where necessary.
- Ask questions about why things happen and how they work.
- Build and construct with a wide range of objects, selecting appropriate resources, and adapting their work where necessary.

Physical Development
- Use a range of small and large equipment.
- Handle tools, objects, construction and malleable materials safely and with increasing control.

Creative Development
- Express and communicate their ideas, thoughts and feelings by using a widening range of materials, suitable tools, imaginative and role play, movement, designing and making, and a variety of songs and instruments.
- Respond in a variety of ways to what they see, hear, smell, touch, feel.
- Explore colour, texture, shape, form and space in two and three dimensions.

 # Explanation/discussion

You may need to explore how you feel about mess, your own attitudes and anxieties. It is easy to inhibit children's individual responsibility and initiative by not being clear about how much 'mess' is acceptable. Ask yourself how much the idea of 'order and tidiness' governs what happens in the messy area. Are you prepared to share control with the children in spite of the potential for chaos? Do you spend time observing how children use materials in order to support further learning, or are you more concerned about keeping things tidy? Are you worried about how your space will appear to premises officers, cleaners, parents?

The effects of untidiness:

The 'messy play area' can cause anxiety to some practitioners, who only see its potential for untidiness. Their response is to place a tight rein on the children's actions, but this will only curtail exploration, experimentation and learning. These practitioners will probably spend most of their time going round after the children tidying up. In your team, you need to agree the difference between productive and creative mess, and an untidy shambles. While the former is stimulating and exciting the latter is no use to anybody and gets in the way of learning. Activities like woodwork can cause anxieties, but many of these are alleviated when procedures are agreed by the staff team, and clearly understood by the children. Some activities require a minimum level of staffing. On occasions when there are not enough staff, we need to tell the children that these activities are not available, and why. This could be done simply by covering the woodwork table with a drape, or displaying a symbol that conveys the same message.

Mess can cause anxiety!

Procedures can be misunderstood!

Some activities are off the menu!

Protection not restriction!

The importance of organised settings:

The organisation of resources is also extremely important. In many settings staff decide what will be available to the children each day. This may mean that the children get the opportunity to use a wide range of resources, but it can also result in them being unable to think independently and use what they need at the time they most need it. If we are truly committed to the development of children's independence and initiative, then it is they who should decide what is to be used to facilitate their own learning. This demands that practitioners are prepared to lose some of the control – and also that they are extremely well organised!

Organisation encourages independent thinking!

Case Study - Messy Activities

A group of parents had volunteered to transform an uninteresting piece of grass into a sensory garden. The project was going extremely well and some of the children were really enjoying being involved in planning the garden and making the preparations. The final plan involved the removal of some turf and the laying of foundations for raised flower beds. As the children helped with the digging they discovered some smooth, white, round stones that they were convinced were dinosaur eggs.

One of the diggers, Adam, suggested that it would be a good idea to bury the eggs in the sand so that they could hatch. He collected the stones and made off for the sand tray. Several others followed, and it was not long before all the stones had been buried.

"Why don't we put some dinosaurs in the sand as well?" suggested Trevor.

It was agreed that this would be a good idea, and Trevor headed off to the storage shelf, returning a few moments later with a box of plastic dinosaurs. For the next few minutes the small group of children became engrossed in arranging the dinosaurs in the sand tray.

Mrs Turner, who was supervising the room, had been watching carefully. Bending down beside the sand tray she began to question the children, to find out what they already knew about dinosaurs, where they had lived, what they ate and how they moved. As a result of this conversation the children decided that they needed some trees for the dinosaurs. They thought they would probably be able to find some in the garden, so Mrs Turner fetched the secateurs and they all went outside. The children selected the foliage they needed to make trees in the sand tray and hurried back inside to put them in place. This was easier said than done as the foliage kept toppling over in the dry sand.

"We need to wet the sand to make them stand up right!" announced Sarah. She picked up a bucket and hurried over to the sink. After wetting and packing the sand the foliage stood up much better and the children seemed pleased with the results.

While all this had been happening, Adam had been to the book corner to fetch a book about dinosaurs. When he returned he had the book open at the middle page where there was a stunning dinosaur picture. "Look" he said, "we need some stones, there's lots of rocks in this picture!"

"We could get them from outside," suggested Trevor, and once again everyone went back outside for a stone hunt. There were plenty of large, lumpy stones but they were muddy, so the children decided to wash them in the sink. Eva filled the sink with water and the stones were soon cleaned and ready to be added to the diorama in the sand tray. As the children carried them away, Trevor remained. For him the fascination of the water on the stones surpassed the appeal of the dinosaur scene!

We Can Do It!

Case Study CONCLUSION

This example of **messy activities** illustrates how giving children ownership can energise them and unlock their creative potential. Think how much more the children have learnt here, with Mrs Turner as a sensitive observer and facilitator, than if they had simply been instructed and given materials to make a dinosaur scene.

Quality CHECKLIST ✓

Ask yourself –

- As a staff team, have we spent time looking at how we ensure safe, enjoyable play?
- Do we have a shared understanding of what we mean by 'mess'? Have we talked about mess v. tidiness, so that we are all more or less in agreement about what is acceptable and what is not?
- Can we all tell the difference between creative and uncreative mess?
- Could we involve the children more in the management and maintenance of the messy areas?
- Are there enough opportunities for children to pursue messy activities outside?
- Do we make sure that boys and girls are given equal encouragement and opportunity to participate in these aspects of work?
- Do we encourage parents and children to contribute ideas, experiences, resources and expertise?
- Do we have enough resources for these activities? Are our resources high quality and 'fit for the purpose?'

We Can Do It!

Resources for messy activities

Many of the resources for messy activities are easily available in your setting. Dough, gloop, cornflour, paste, water, sand, gravel are used regularly and are the basis of the most popular activities. These simple resources can be supplemented by adding more unusual substances such as shaving foam or additives to familiar ones – try adding glitter to sand.

For messy activities you will need:

- Flexible storage so children know where to find things, but also feel free to mix and combine things.

- Protective clothing is essential for messy play. This should be comfortable, well organised and easy to put on (or they won't bother!). Old shirts worn back to front, teeshirts or old fashioned aprons are sometimes more useful than the stiff plastic school aprons. Goggles should be provided for woodwork and children encouraged to wear them.

- Dough, sand and water appear regularly in most settings. Spice these up by adding a surprise element such as glitter, buried objects, paste or ice.

- Consider how you could include some more unusual substances such as clay, finger paint, mud, shaving foam, ice, jelly, cooked pasta to extend and enrich the children's experiences.

- Tools and other equipment also need careful attention and storage. Try vegetable racks, wall hooks, plastic baskets so that children can get out and put resources away themselves.

- Display wrapping papers, pictures of sculptures and other 3-D artefacts along with examples of textures from natural and man-made sources.

- Use painting programmes to encourage freedom in creativity.

Use photocopies and computer print outs in collage and construction.

- Take digital photos of messy activities in progress, as the process is often more valuable than the outcome!

Make sound tapes of junk music and home-made sound makers.

We Can Do It!

Getting messy!

- Instead of putting out resources for the children **ask**, 'What do you plan to do in the sand/water/modelling area, and so on, today? What things do you think you will need?'.
- **Tune in** to what they are currently interested in and reflect these interests in the resources and materials you provide and the discussions you initiate.
- Have **'themed'** boxes for sand and water play. Talk with the children about what they think should go in the boxes.
- Let the children take **responsibility** for filling and emptying the water tray.
- Encourage the children to mix their own dough. Let them **decide** what colour, texture or smell they would like it to have.
- **Involve** the children in choosing and ordering new equipment.
- Train them to use a **camera** so that they can photograph projects that have gone particularly well.
- Observe and note the **conversations** going on between children. Use these as starting points for discussions, new resources and changes.
- Use storylines, objects and characters to **inspire play**, by linking messy play with stories, for example *Where the Wild Things Are*; *The Rainbow Fish* and traditional tales such as *The Gingerbread Man*.
- Encourage children to use **resources from other areas** with the sand, water and malleable materials – small world models and figures can give real life and vigour to the play. Let them use constructions made in the woodwork area in the sand and water, incorporate figures made with clay or dough in brick play.
- Spend time **observing** the way children are using the materials.
- Put up posters in the sand, water, dough and woodwork areas that promote discussion and give the children **ideas** for things they could try out.
- Bury some **'treasure'** in the sand for the children to discover, for example some old coins in a small treasure box, or a bundle of old keys.
- Invite **visitors** to talk about their work, for example. potters, carpenters, cooks. They don't have to be professionals.
- Make sure that these areas are resourced with appropriate information **books**.
- Refer children's ideas to other children so that they can gain **inspiration from each other**.
- Add **smells, textures and sparkle** to dough by using glitter, sequins, rice, colour, aromatherapy oils, and so on.
- Add **unusual things** to the water tray, such as ice cubes with sequins or flowers frozen in them.
- Use **different things** in the sand and water trays such as noodles (cooked or uncooked), spaghetti, bark, compost, pebbles, gravel, lentils, slime, porridge.

Try these activities as starters...

- Spray shaving foam on a plastic topped table. Add a squirt of ready mixed paint.
- Dig a slice of turf (and its soil) and put it in a sand tray or builder's tray. Offer trowels, or old spoons and forks for exploring.
- Fill your water tray with jelly.
- Provide a box of wood offcuts (free from a wood yard) and white glue.

Sound & Movement

> "Music is a form of communication that is spiritual, emotional and intellectual. The steady pulse of the body, the rhythm of steps, the heart beat, means that the rhythm of music is natural to us."
>
> Bernadette Duffy in 'Supporting Creativity and Imagination in the Early Years'

Introduction

Movement and sound enable children to develop skills, concepts and attitudes in a range of contexts. They provide opportunities for creativity and imagination, language, social observation, listening, attention skills, memory, counting and mathematical skills, concentration... and much, much more. And when the children are able to take on some of the responsibility for organising their own experiences then the learning is truly enhanced.

In the best practice adults provide the resources and introduce activities that enable the children to see their potential. Adults then take a back seat and allow the children to explore in their own way. At this point they need sensitive support. By observing the ways in which individuals work with the materials, practitioners will be able to judge what other opportunities should be made available, and work out ways to move them on in their explorations.

It is worth remembering that although only a minority of children will become professional dancers and musicians, all children enjoy dancing and making music.

Links with Early Learning Goals

Creative Development

- Explore colour, texture, shape, form and space in two and three dimensions.
- Recognise and explore how sounds can be changed, sing simple songs from memory, recognise repeated sounds and sound patterns, and match movements to music.
- Respond in a variety of ways to what they see, hear, smell, touch, and feel.
- Use their imagination in art and design, music, dance, imaginative role-play, and stories.
- Express and communicate their ideas, thoughts and feelings by using a widening range of materials, suitable tools, imaginative role-play, movement, designing and making, and a variety of songs and musical instruments.

Explanation/discussion

For young children, movement and sound are closely linked. When they hear music they often move to the sound and rhythm. When they are moving and dancing they will frequently make sounds. Children in the Foundation Stage are developing their musical awareness and skills with great speed. They have increasing control over their voices, can play simple rhythm instruments and are beginning to understand concepts of tempo, beat, melody and pitch. They are also starting to enjoy making music as part of a group.

To keep this enthusiasm and enjoyment alive it is essential that there is time for children to engage in musical activities initiated by themselves and their peers. It is important to furnish settings with a rich range of resources with which the children can explore music and sound.

Most children are fascinated by things that make a noise:

- Watch the way they examine and investigate new objects. As well as tasting and feeling they bang and shake to see if any sound results. And when they do find things that can produce a musical note or two, they are delighted.

- Basic timing and a mastery of steady beat are necessary to any task that involves sophisticated movement, and where a person lacks beat awareness he or she usually demonstrates a motor skill deficiency. Many researchers and early years workers are currently interested in the links between early movement experiences and future learning.

- Recent studies show a close link between beat competency and school achievement. Other research suggests that sensory stimulation of the sort provided by movement and dancing has an actual physical effect on the structure of the brain. If true, this has major implications for settings. The opportunities that are provided for movement play, and how children are supported towards 'body awareness' and 'body thinking' become very important. So does how children are taught to 'listen' to bodily-felt experiences.

However, if we hold all the power and control then the children will be denied the opportunity to take a lead in group activities. Children need to be given the chance to make choices and take decisions about which rhymes or songs will be sung, which instruments will be played, how loudly or softly sounds should be made or sung and the tempo at which a piece should be performed. By enjoying being in control they will gain the confidence to repeat experiences on their own.

Case Study – Sound and Movement

The children had been inspired by a dance session lead by Mrs Patel. She had demonstrated a variety of dances from her culture, and then worked with the children with long lengths of beautiful fabric. This session had been met with such enthusiasm that the children's keyworker asked Mrs Patel if it would be possible to borrow the fabric so that they could use it again.

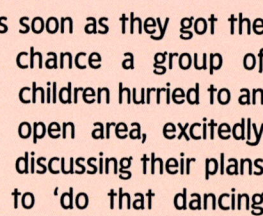

As soon as they got the chance a group of children hurried to an open area, excitedly discussing their plans to 'do that dancing again!'. Yasmin eagerly gave out the material while Thomas went to the CD player to start the music. But although Mrs Patel had been able to lend her fabric to the children she had needed to take the music away with her. Realising what had happened Thomas suggested that they use some other music. They tried three or four alternatives but all agreed that none was suitable. "Why don't we make up our own music?" said Omar. "We could use the instruments!".

The music area was next to the open area. This had been a conscious decision on the part of the practitioners, so that the work in both could overlap. Omar, Jack and Amy rushed over to the instruments and chose tambourines, a small snare drum and a 'rain stick'. After some exploration, and negotiation about who should play what, the 'orchestra' began.
"You're playing too loud!" said Yasmin. "We don't need it that loud!"
After several attempts the noise level was gradually adjusted and the dancers began swaying, swirling and running with their lengths of fabric. This continued for some time until Yasmin, who was emerging as choreographer, began to suggest other ways in which the fabric could be used. So the dance developed. All joined in except Omar, who insisted on doing his own thing.
"Look, he's spoiling it," said Jack. "He won't do it right.".

With sensitive intervention from the keyworker the problem was resolved so that Omar's movement sequence became an extension of the dance. This resulted in other children wanting to do the same until the dance became quite long.
"Its great," exclaimed Yasmin. "If we practised we could do it for everybody at circle time." Everyone agreed, and after a few more rehearsals the children hurried away to the writing area to make posters and tickets for their performance.

Case Study — CONCLUSION

This is an example of work with **movement and sound**, which balances child and adult initiated learning. Mrs Patel demonstrated the importance of music to her culture, and the children's extension of the experience was sensitively supported by their practitioners. Time should be given to introducing independent use of CD players, musical instruments and other equipment. Older children can demonstrate the proper and careful use of such equipment to younger children.

Quality CHECKLIST ✓

Ask yourself –

- How much do we value music, dance and movement play? How do we show that they are valued?
- How and how well do we support the development of 'body intelligence'? Is our setting organised and equipped for movement play?
- Do we encourage the children to contribute ideas, experiences and resources for music and movement work?
- Are there enough opportunities for the children to compose their own music, sound sequences and dances?
- Are there enough opportunities for children to perform music and dance?
- Are the children able to watch others perform? (Children learn by listening, watching and copying.)
- Is there enough space for children to play instruments and move freely, without disturbing others?
- Are there recycled materials available which the children can use to make musical instruments?
- Have the children been taught how to care for the resources?

Do you –

- move with the children?
- notice and observe children moving?
- create situations which invite movement?
- plan activities that focus on movement, sensation and feelings?
- use the language of movement?
- support children in taking the lead in movement activities?

Resources for sound and movement

Make live and recorded music a regular part of your day and week. Accompany singing sessions, make your own sound makers and musical instruments. If space is a problem, make music outside, put up a curtain or screen, or have loud and quiet days. Store instruments and equipment on open shelves or trolleys, so children can help themselves to the things they need. All electrical equipment and musical instruments should be checked regularly for safety and hygiene.

Create a music area

- Make collections of tapes and CDs so that the children can listen to a wide range of music from a variety of cultures.
- Share control with the children, allowing them to take the lead, as and when they feel ready.
- Make a collection of objects that make a noise.
- Set up a 'performance area' where children can go to perform musical pieces, movement sequences and dances – it could easily be outside.
- Provide a range of objects, fabrics and artifacts to support children's movement ideas, for example scarves, ribbon sticks, lengths of material, hoops, beanbags, and so on.
- Set up a music area with instruments where children can go to compose their own musical pieces.
- Create a listening corner where children can choose music they would like to hear.
- Provide a tape recorder so that children can tape their own music.
- Display pictures of musicians, dancers, singers from all cultures and types of music.
- Do not forget the important place popular music, TV themes and advertising jingles have in children's lives. Include these in your selections through tape and video.
- Drape fabric and soft furnishings to absorb sound as well as make the area more welcoming.

- Provide keyboards and other electronic musical instruments.
- Give access to simple tape recorders that children can operate themselves.
- Try Colour Step games where the footpads or stepping stones make sounds.
- Offer personal stereos and headphones for music on the move.
- Make the CD player child friendly so they can put their own music on.
- Use musical toys as stimuli for stories and listening activities.
- Have a karaoke session!

ICT Box

We Can Do It!

Getting moving!

- Set up a **music area** where children can use instruments and make music throughout the day.

- Play a **wide variety** of music and encourage the children to talk about their favourite pieces and why they like them. Have a listening centre where children can listen to different kinds of music. Allow them to choose some of the music.

- **Sing** with and for the children. **Dance** with and for the children. Be enthusiastic in your response to their singing, movement and dancing.

- **Allow time** for children to build on what they have heard and seen modelled.

- Develop their '**body intelligence**' by encouraging children to be aware of all the different ways in which their bodies will move.

- Introduce the children to **new instruments**. You don't have to be an expert in playing them yourself – just able to raise a sound! Ask questions which will steer the children into offering ideas about how they could be used.

- **Invite the children to choose** which songs they would most like to sing. Encourage them to have fun with language by making up their own songs, rhymes and jingles.

- Make collections of **different things** that children can move with, and let them decide the 'what with and how' for the movement session. Encourage them to compose their own musical movement sequences and dances. Model the possibilities and then let them take the lead. Look for something to value in every effort.

- **Use stories** as starting points for music and movement.

- Compose '**sound pictures**' – let the children decide the focus, for example the zoo, park, seaside, forest, etc. – and encourage them to discuss various ways of making the sounds.

- Arrange for the children to hear **adults and older children** singing, playing instruments and dancing.

Musical ideas for starters...

- Leave a basket of simple instruments by the outside door to encourage music in the garden.
- Tie objects such as saucepan lids, tins, spoons, trays to fences and railings. Add some short sticks for beaters so children can make 'Junk Music'.
- Try playing music to indicate activity changes during the day – a lively march, a gentle song, a tune to clap to.

Outdoor Play

"Where possible, practitioners should allow children to move spontaneously between indoor and outdoor environments. Children will improve their co-ordination, control and ability to move more effectively if they can run, climb, balance, swing, slide, tumble, throw, catch and kick when they want to and are motivated and interested in doing so."

QCA - Guidance for the Foundation Stage

Introduction

Outdoor play is an entitlement for all children in the Foundation Stage. Nowadays parents are worried about safety and want to keep their children within sight, so that for many the chance to play in the garden or the park is rare. Many homes don't have much space for energetic outdoor play. This means that children often grow up with few opportunities to play outdoors, and many have no contact with their friends at the end of the day or at weekends. In addition, extended periods of uninterrupted physical activity are less common, even inside our settings. Use the ideas in this chapter to help you to redress the balance.

Links with Early Learning Goals

Personal and social development
- Continue to be interested, excited and motivated to learn.
- Respond to significant experiences, showing a range of feelings when appropriate.
- Work harmoniously as part of a group or class, taking turns and sharing fairly, with agreed values and codes of behaviour for groups of people, including adults and children.
- Select and use activities and resources independently.

Language, communication and literacy
- Use language to imagine and recreate roles and experiences.
- Interact with others, negotiating plans and activities and taking turns in conversations.
- Attempt writing for various purposes, using different forms such as lists, stories, instructions.
- Write their own names and labels and form sentences, sometimes using punctuation.

Mathematical
- Use everyday words to describe position.

Knowledge and Understanding of the World
- Find out about, and identify some features of living things, objects and events they observe.
- Ask questions about why things happen and how things work.
- Build and construct with a wide range of objects, selecting appropriate resources, and adapting their work where necessary.
- Observe, find out and identify features in the natural world.

Physical Development
- Move with confidence, imagination and in safety.
- Move with control and co-ordination.
- Show awareness of space, of themselves and others.
- Use a range of small and large equipment.
- Travel around, under, over and through balancing and climbing equipment.

Explanation/discussion

The Guidance for the Foundation Stage recommends that practitioners 'plan activities which offer appropriate physical challenges, provide sufficient space, indoors and outdoors to set up relevant activities, give sufficient time for children to use a range of equipment' and 'use additional adult help to support individuals and to encourage increased independence in physical activities'.

Playing with friends and having fun (particularly outside) is one of the things young children place in their top three favourites. Outdoor play should offer the right sort of challenges, with space and time to develop their ideas, good resources and supportive adults. However, across settings there is a wide range of outdoor play provision, and some children do not get the experiences they need.

Social play:

Outdoor play also gives endless opportunities for social play: learning how to negotiate, co-operate and share equipment and games, how to work in a group, to take turns, to delay their own gratification in the interests of others.

Apparatus:

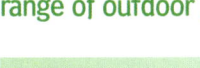

Large apparatus and wheeled toys encourage **physical development and the co-ordination** of eye, ear, hand and foot. The use of small apparatus refines motor skills – throwing, catching, bouncing, rolling – and the chance to run, jump, hop, roll, skip, push and pull give the chance to enjoy space and freedom.

Activities and equipment usually reserved for indoors – mark-making, writing, books and other table top activities – can appear in trays, on rugs or on tables. We can provide **quiet areas and wild areas**.

We can encourage interest in the **natural environment** and its care by offering weather watching, sensory gardens, flowers, bird tables and small ponds. Paint, dough, sand, woodwork and other messy materials can be available. Small world, farm, jungle and zoo animals and vehicles all have a place, where chalk or paint can provide instant roads, fields and enclosures.

Cost effectiveness:

Providing outdoor play does not have to be an expensive exercise. Tents, gazebos and plastic furniture are all easy to find, and at the end of the summer can often be picked up cheaply. As well as sales in supermarkets and garden centres, look for second-hand items in newspapers and shop windows. Guttering, rope, cardboard and wooden boxes, pieces of fabric and clips for fixing them, playground chalk, clipboards and materials for signs and labels cost little and will relieve the pressure on more expensive wheeled toys and fixed apparatus.

Case Study – Outdoor Play

Brendon walks towards the outside door, which opens onto the patio area and the garden. As he passes Nazia, he says, "Coming outside?". Nazia looks up from the train track, nods and joins him, bringing the train with her. The two children pause on the threshold to the garden. They look round to see what is going on outside. It is autumn, and although it is sunny the gusting wind sets the wind chimes ringing and swirls leaves across the garden. It feels cold.

"I'm getting my coat," says Brendon. "Do you want yours?" He fetches their coats and they put them on.

The play area is busy. Bikes are popular, and a small group of children run with ribbons streaming from their hands in the wind. A basket of bean bags, small balls and quoits has been placed just outside the door. A small trolley with playground chalk, clipboards and mark makers is also at hand. A pop-up tent has been erected on the edge of the grass, with a prop basket containing lengths of fabric, assorted hats and bags and an old mobile phone. Another mobile phone is 'in use' at the top of the climbing frame.

Nazia runs back inside and soon reappears with some bubbles, which she and Brendon begin to blow. Other children come to join the game, jumping and racing to catch the bubbles. Ben (a Nursery Nurse) has been watching. He begins to talk about the colours in the bubbles and the way they are swept away by the wind. The children stand still and watch, commenting on what is happening.

After a while Brendon and Nazia give the bubbles to another child and go over to the edge of the hard playground, where leaves have been blown into a pile by the wind. They pick up leaves and throw them into the air, watching as they fly. Some sycamore seeds have also blown into the garden. Brendon knows about these.

"My dad calls these helicopters," he says. "Look how they fly." He shows Nazia how to throw the seeds, and both children toss the seeds into the air, watching them spin and twirl. Brendon puts some seeds in his pocket to show the other children later.

Nazia says, "I'm thirsty. I'm getting a drink. Are you coming?"

Brendon shakes his head. "I'm going in the sand."

Nazia fetches a drink from inside and brings it to the picnic table on the patio. She sits and watches

the other children, content for a few minutes to just observe their play.

Meanwhile Brendon, Jake and Carly are building an animal park in the sand tray. They make cages for the animals with small sticks from the ground, and fetch some card from the trolley to make a notice for the park.

A child rings a small bell to warn that it is time to pack up the toys. Everybody helps to collect the bikes, to return balls and quoits to the basket, to clean the blackboards which are fixed to the fence, and to untie the ribbons from the tree branches. Brendon takes the 'helicopter' seeds out of his pocket and sends one flying before going inside to join the group for a story.

Case Study CONCLUSION

This is a good example of **outdoor play** where children were confident. They knew what they wanted to do and had ideas about how to do it. They respected each other, listened to each other and worked together collaboratively. There was space for children to take time out to watch what was going on. At clearing up time they worked as a team to put things away and prepare for the end of the session.

Quality CHECKLIST ✓

Ask yourself –

- Is our outdoor area an exciting, flexible environment? Does it change frequently to meet the needs of the children and give them opportunities in all areas of learning?
- Are the children encouraged to change and adapt the outdoor areas, furniture, equipment, and so on?
- Could the children be more involved in selecting and buying new equipment and apparatus?
- Do we consider versatility when choosing new equipment, making sure that new things have many possible uses, that they can be used by more than one child at a time, that children of different ages and stages can use them?
- Is the outdoor storage accessible to the children? Can they help to get things out and put them away? Do children use the sheds or other outdoor storage spaces when they are empty? Are we making the best use of all our space?
- Could we involve them more in deciding what goes out and where?
- Do we give opportunities for children to personalise their play by, for example, offering flexible resources with many uses and providing mark-making equipment?
- Do we regularly watch children playing in this area to find out how we can enhance and extend the quality of their play?

We Can Do It!

Resources for outdoor play

If children are encouraged to get out their own apparatus and equipment, from trolleys, sheds, baskets and boxes, they will always use it more imaginatively than if we decide for them. They will combine, adapt and interpret simple objects such as ropes, posts, screens and signs in many and varied ways. They will improvise from given materials to make others. They will use static equipment to support and extend temporary structures, and they will incorporate wheeled toys into their play, improving daily on what they have done before. They will bring the inside out and the outside in – if we give them ownership of their play.

Create fun outdoor areas with:

- Wicker baskets and boxes with handles for props, picnics, role play.
- Laundry baskets for bricks and small world toys. Make sure they are light enough for the children to carry.
- Small trolleys or stacking vegetable baskets keep small things like balls and bean bags safe. They are also useful for outside collage, paint, sand toys, science stuff, garden tools.
- Child-sized bags and baskets are good for clearing up. Have several so all the children can help.
- Pop-up tents and gazebos make great portable shelters.
- Barrels, tyres, boxes, planks and tubes cost little and encourage imagination.
- Small containers with different sets (dinosaurs, people, farm/zoo animals, cars and so on) can be used by the children in different places (sand, water, table top, grass).
- Small versions of metal garden tools, brushes, pans, spades and so on are much more rewarding than plastic.
- Put hooks and shelves in your shed, so things can hang up. Paint pictures of the objects and put by the relevant hook, so they can be put back in the right places.

- Try a cheap set of walkie talkies.
- Use the video camera to record some of those active sessions, children love seeing themselves.
- Show the children how to use the digital camera or occasionally give them disposable cameras to record their view of what's important to them.
- Offer mobile phones (take the batteries out first).
- Show children how to access gardening websites to look at flowers and choose plants for the garden (www.bbc.co.uk/gardening).
- Use the computer to make flags, pennants, labels, posters and notices.

ICT Box

We Can Do It!

# Getting Started Outdoors!

- **Don't put everything out** for the children. Encourage them to be involved in what goes out and where.
- Boxes, planks, ropes, buckets and pulleys will give more **scope for imagination** than fixed apparatus. Watch for their ideas to emerge and encourage them.
- Encourage children to **name and label their structures**. Make sure there are plenty of opportunities for them to make their own signs, notices, flags, instructions, labels, badges, and so on.
- **Involve** the children in choosing the location and timing of snacks and drinks, stories, circle time.
- When you buy, involve the children. Ask them what they need, **let them help** with choosing new equipment and resources.
- Let the children **choose what to grow,** and don't be afraid to let them experiment. You might not be able to grow bananas in Barking but you could let children plant seeds outdoors and indoors to see what happens. If you haven't got a garden, let them plant and care for seeds or bulbs in pots, window boxes and containers.
- Screw white or blackboards to the wall or fence. Make some of them big for **collaborative work**.
- **Put up a batten** of wood along a wall or fence, about a metre or so from the ground. Pin paper or card to the batten for painting, chalk or crayons.
- Offer a **basket of playground chalk** for games and drawing pictures. Let them draw on patio slabs, the rain will wash the pictures away.
- Use some lightweight fabrics and clips or clothes pegs to **make some screens**. See how the children react.
- **Plan some surprises** to promote language and exploration – for example a mirror, bubbles, streamers, footprints, a basket of new objects.

Outdoor ideas for starters...

- Hang a basket in a tree or bush (or from the top of a climbing frame).
- Have a day (or a week) with no wheeled toys.
- Take a nursery rhyme or singing games tape outside.
- Leave a small basket of labels, pens and masking tape on a table.
- Scrounge some carpet samples or offcuts to sit on.
- Have a pop-up tent out in the rain.

We Can Do It!

R⁰le Play

> "**Children will learn** to explore, express and communicate their ideas and use their imaginations when they have sufficient time to research their ideas, imitate what they see, experiment with ideas and bring their own ideas to the process."
>
> *QCA, Curriculum Guidance for the Foundation Stage*

 ## Introduction

Role play is a vital part of children's education in the Foundation Stage and beyond. It forms the basis for story telling, writing and social development and gives opportunities for children to play out the events they observe and experience. It provides experience of real life situations in which they can practise their learning, and develop their creativity – but above all it is fun!

 ## Links with Early Learning Goals

Almost all the Early Learning Goals can be addressed through role play. However, these are the key ones:

- Interact with others, negotiating plans and taking turns in conversation (Communication, Language and Literacy).
- Listen and respond to stories and songs (Communication, Language and Literacy).
- Extend vocabulary (Communication, Language and Literacy).
- Use language to imagine and recreate roles and experiences, organise, sequence and clarify thinking, ideas, feelings and events (Communication, Language and Literacy).
- Use their imagination in imaginative and role play and stories (Creative Development).

 ## Explanation/discussion

Role play offers endless opportunities to learn. Imaginative children may sometimes enjoy solitary role play, but social interaction, taking turns and sharing are an important part of this type of play. This makes it less easy than most to play on your own.

To experience stories in action through your imagination (giants, bears, divers, heroes, astronauts) provides a springboard to narrative in prose and poetry and unlocks children's creativity. How can you write an adventure story if you have never had an adventure? How can you describe the feelings of fictional characters unless you have practised them in role?

But role play is not just about superheroes. It has a contribution to the understanding of more 'ordinary' life by offering children opportunities to explore the

roles of adults in the real world. Skills such as using the 'phone, making meals, shopping, taking care of others can all be practised in role, without anxiety or threat. A range of cultures and contexts can be used as situations for role play, opening the door to the lives and lifestyles of the families in the local area by using implements, wearing clothes, eating food of other cultures and countries. Writing in role when making lists, labels, letters and appointments or taking names, allows children to practise their emergent writing and helps to reinforce the functions and importance of writing. Counting things, checking, selling, buying give opportunities to become aware of numbers and their uses. Negotiating and compromising give practice in social skills.

There are three major types of role play:

Domestic Play...
...where the home and family are at the centre, with the normal routines of everyday life. The situations explored – such as cleaning, cooking, eating, sleeping – may be familiar or new. We should aim for a varied range, some rooted in the children's own experience, some encouraging flights of fancy and imagination. Try a barbecue or a country cottage, a caravan or a lighthouse, a giant's house or a palace. Remember that there are opportunities outside as well as those indoors.

Transactional Play...
...where goods, services and advice are exchanged for money. These are endlessly fascinating to children, probably because transactions are a major part of what they observe of adult behaviour. You can include shops, travel agents, vets, clinics, markets, garden centres and many others.

Imagined Worlds...
...those places where stories dwell, or places the children are less likely to have visited – such as under the sea, a cave, a jungle. For city children the seaside may be an imagined world; for country children it may be a tower block. Some children may have travelled several times on an aeroplane but never on a bus. To some the dark is familiar, to others it is frightening and unknown. Give children the chance to come to terms with the unfamiliar by exploring it in their imaginations through role play.

All three types of play can be provided in a variety of ways: through 'whole body' play, dressing up and using life-sized equipment (or replicas); through 'small world' play using toys such as Lego or Playmobil; and through the use of puppets, dolls or figures. A play setting outside could link with a domestic setting inside. For instance, outside there could be a train or bus, inside there could be a hospital, a shop or a garden centre. If you can offer more than one of these types of play at the same time, the results will be deeper, more complex, more intense, and will offer the children richer experiences.

Case Study – Role Play

Mrs Senga, who helps in the classroom, came to school having just had her hair permed. The children were fascinated by her curls and followed her everywhere, intrigued by the new look. Mrs Senga and some of the children went to the school library but they couldn't find a book about hairdressing. At group time, Mrs Senga was asked to describe what had happened at the hairdressers. The children asked some very complex questions. Mrs Brennigan, their teacher, decided that a visit was indicated and on her way home she called at a local hairdresser's and asked if they could cope with a class visit.

A few days later the children walked along the road for the visit. They had already talked about the hairdresser and had some ideas of what they wanted to see and ask. The hairdresser had arranged to do a free wash and set for a local customer so that the children could take careful note of how the rollers and drier were used. Some children made picture lists on clipboards. Mrs Senga was in charge of the digital camera and some of the children took 'photos. The hairdresser gave each child a shampoo sample to take home and a big bag of rollers, brushes, shoulder capes and an appointment book. For their role play during the next few days, the children brought things from home to complete the preparations – magazines, an old hairdryer (with the flex removed), a telephone handset, empty hairspray and shampoo bottles. They also collected bowls, towels, pens and paper, purses and money. They made a price list, which included haircuts for the dolls. They put up posters and made a style book of pictures from magazines. The 'photos from the visit were printed and mounted, including a whole series of the process of a 'wash and blow dry'. This really helped with sequencing an unfamiliar event. Chairs, tables, overalls and a booking desk, complete with the 'phone and the appointment book completed the preparations. The children decided to call their shop 'Hair Do', and with Mrs Senga's help they made a big sign to go on the door.

The boys were just as keen to be involved as the girls, both as hairdressers and as clients. Visitors brought dolls from the home play area, members of staff were invited to make appointments, and parents called in . The children took 'photos of their 'salon' to send with letters of thanks for their visit. Every child in the class became involved and even the most withdrawn children took part, growing in confidence. The children often adopted their parents' names when they made appointments. Their technical language and the language of transactional situations became very sophisticated, and this affected other activities in the classroom.

The concentrated play lasted for several weeks, until a spell of really fine weather stimulated interest in the school garden and the children decided to dismantle the hairdresser's and use the equipment to set up a garden centre outside.

Case Study — CONCLUSION

This is an example of **role play** of a very high quality. These children were completely involved in setting up and organising their own learning environment. The practitioners followed the interests of the children and responded positively to the leads which they gave. They watched and listened, were sensitive to the things children were interested in, and offered resources to support them. They used these starting points to extend children's learning through first-hand experiences, play and talk. This in turn stimulated the imagination and creativity of the children, and gave them wonderful opportunities to develop the skills of independent learning.

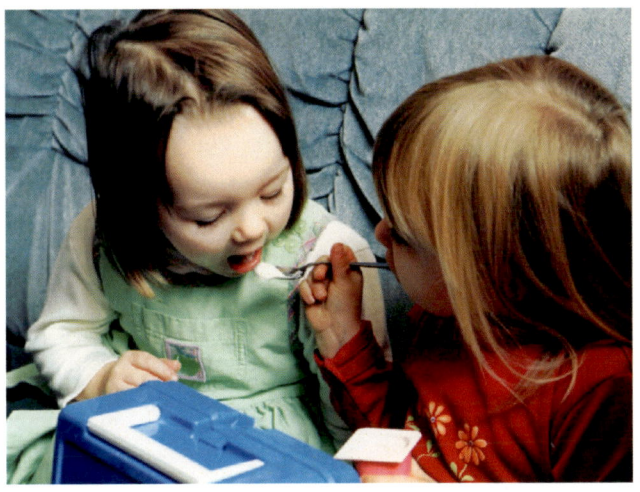

Quality CHECKLIST ✓

Role play is a powerful learning tool, which should never be devalued by poor provision. In settings where the staff and children are used to working and planning together, children will be involved in decisions about setting up, location, focus, equipment, the time for change as well as the play itself.

Ask yourself –

- How much independence do we allow our children in role play?
- Do we encourage children to change and adapt the role play areas, furniture, equipment, and so on?
- Could we involve the children more in setting up new areas?
- Are the resources of the highest quality we can afford?
- Do role play activities and resources reflect the groups and communities living in the area, and the backgrounds of the children in our setting? Do they offer opportunities for children to broaden their experience?
- Do we change the role play areas often enough?
- Have we considered the benefits of more than one role play area?
- Is role play on offer outdoors as well as inside our setting?
- Are there opportunities for informal and spontaneous role play as well as for play in more permanent settings?
- Do we provide role play clothing and resources which are likely to appeal to both genders? Do we encourage children away from gender stereotyping in their play? Is there equivalence between genders in both indoor and outdoor play?
- Do we encourage parents and children to contribute ideas, experiences and resources for role play?

Resources for role play

Build up collections, boxes or baskets on different themes. They could include a story sack with a book and all the props for acting it out. Children need access to more (or more complicated) equipment for transactional play than for domestic or imagined play. Parents or local traders can often help with larger equipment. There is much reasonably priced children's furniture in garden centres and shops.

These are useful:

- Easy to move, lightweight furniture and screens.
- Well organised hanging space for clothes – hooks and loops on garments.
- Unisex, all purpose tabards or overalls (these are easy to make).
- A small bench and a mirror near a dressing up area.
- Magazines, newspapers, leaflets and forms.
- Telephones (mobile and fixed) – the more you have, the more they will talk!
- Light fabrics that can be tied or clipped to furniture, trees and static equipment to make tents and shelters – or to tie round heads or bodies.
- Hats and headbands, stickers and badges.
- Playground chalk for markings.
- Flags, streamers, shop signs, banners.
- White boards or blackboards on fences, walls and outside structures with pens or chalk.
- Baskets, picnic sets, mats and blankets for picnics.
- Plastic cones, crates and guttering.
- Materials for making signs, notices, badges.
- Post boxes, road signs, traffic lights, steering wheels.
- A range of items from different ethnic and social backgrounds.

ICT Box

- Use a microwave instead of a conventional oven.
- Try one or more mobile phones (batteries removed first).
- Offer dummy or real computers and keyboards in offices and shops.
- Include calculators for shopping or tickets.
- Use television and video remotes (real or home made).
- Digital clocks and watches.
- Make some radios and 'walkie talkies'.
- Make and print shopping lists and make labels and notices.
- Take, print and label digital 'photos; make 'photo albums.
- Make screens, dials and buttons for cockpits and dashboards of vehicles.
- Provide credit cards as well as money for shopping.
- Make or buy some crossing signs or traffic lights.

We Can Do It!

Getting started with role playing!

- If children are to be confident in leading the development of the play they must feel ownership. **Encourage them to make decisions.** For example – start the session by saying, "Where shall we put the house today?"

- Set up a **minimal shop**, office or other setting and wait for them to ask for additional things.

- **Put up a sign**, picture or label to suggest role play ('WINDOW CLEANER', 'GARAGE', 'CAVE'); ask the children what they need to make the place work.

- Put a **prop basket** or box of items on the carpet or outside (cloths and brushes for a car wash; a doctor's kit and white coat; a trowel, fork and some seed packets) and see what happens.

- As soon as a play area becomes stale or uninteresting, ask the children what you should do. **Follow their lead**.

- Discuss purchases of **new equipment**. Let them look at catalogues and books to choose items.

- When you set up a new area or topic, make a list with them and **take them shopping**.

- After a visit, discuss how they can help to set up the **new situation**, where it should be, what it should contain.

- Observe and note the **conversations** going on in the role play areas. Use these as starting points for discussions, new resources and changes.

- **Brainstorm** role play following a story or other stimulus, or at the beginning of a new topic.

- Use **walks and visits** to discuss the jobs people do, shops and services.

- **Invite visitors** – the health visitor, dentist, parents to talk about their jobs.

- **Collect** books and leaflets about jobs.

- Use items of clothing, hats, objects to start conversations about **characters**.

- Use video clips, photos, magazine articles, posters as **starting points**.

- Start a **collection of stories** to stimulate role play and add simple props or make prop boxes or bags.

Try these locations as starters...

- A house and a food shop.
- A cave and a giant's castle.
- A garage and a car wash.
- A hairdressers and a wedding.
- A house with a baby and a baby clinic.
- A garden centre and a café.
- An office and a train.
- A fish and chip shop and a house.
- An aeroplane and a travel agent.

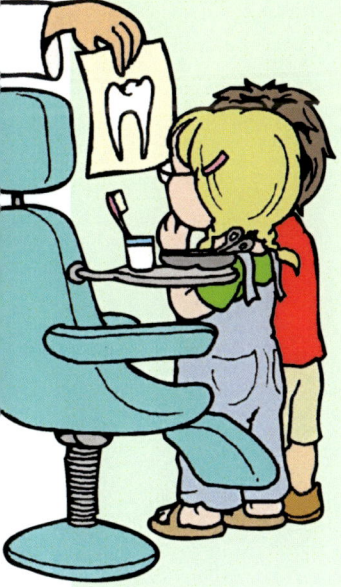

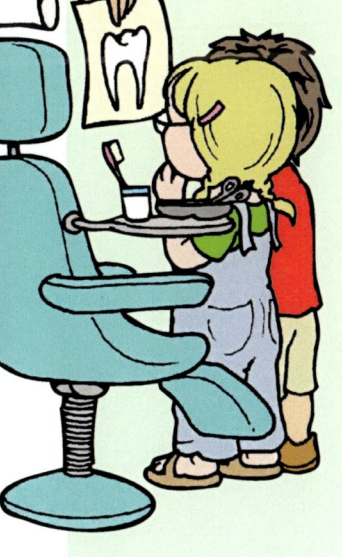

We Can Do It!

Stories

> "Stories are fundamental to human experience, and stories experienced in early childhood can extend children's thinking, foster new knowledge and validate their emotions."
>
> Cathy Nutbrown in 'Threads of Thinking'

Introduction

Stories are of vital importance in the development of young children. When children listen to a story they engage in an active process that impacts on their thinking and influences their perceptions of themselves and the world in which they live. Early years practitioners need to ensure that children have the opportunity to experience a wide range of stories. As children engage with the characters they explore the experiences of others and begin to relate what is happening to others to situations or feelings they have experienced themselves.

Links with Early Learning Goals

Language, Communication and Literacy

- Enjoy listening to and using spoken and written language, and readily turn to it in their play and learning.
- Explore and experiment with sounds, words and texts.
- Listen with enjoyment and respond to stories, songs and other music, rhymes and poems and make up their own stories, songs, rhymes.
- Use language to imagine and recreate roles and experiences.
- Use talk to organise, sequence and clarify thinking, ideas, feelings and events.
- Sustain attentive listening, responding to what they have heard by relevant comments, questions or actions.
- Extend their vocabulary, exploring the meanings and sounds of new words.
- Retell narratives in the correct sequence, drawing on the language patterns of stories.

Explanation/discussion

Stories communicate messages, make statements about right and wrong, suggest ways of going about things and set up expectations. Stories have the potential to profoundly influence the way children behave.

Wherever we go we can see storytelling in action: in shops, cafés, bars, on buses and on street corners, people are telling their stories. Storytelling is a vital part of life and relationships. Stories assist us in learning more about who we are. As we experience them we make sense of things that have happened to us, refine our judgements, modify our point of view and reflect upon our values. It is through our stories that we learn about ourselves, and the world in which we live. This is even more important for children than it is for adults. Stories have great potential for enhancing children's self-knowledge and self-esteem.

Choosing the right stories:

When we choose stories for young children we must think about the messages that we are transmitting. If children are exposed to a diet of stories where the heroes and heroines sit about waiting for someone else to take responsibility for sorting out their problems, this can influence the way they themselves respond to problems and difficulties. If, on the other hand, the stories they hear feature strong, empowered characters ready and willing to take responsibility we may be looking at very different outcomes.

Here's an example:

Cinderella is a victim, picked on by the ugly sisters and exploited by her family. Without the fairy godmother she would have been condemned to a life of drudgery, doomed to live out her days in a dingy basement as a servant to her stepmother and sisters. As she sits, passively accepting her lot, she is powerless. Her destiny is in the hands of her unscrupulous family. She does not expect that life will ever be any different, and when a handsome prince whisks her away no-one is more surprised than she.

But if we were to write the sequel to this story, what might happen to poor Cinderella, disempowered as she is? Suppose the prince fell on hard times and took up with a rich widow as a means of solving his problems – what would become of Cinderella then?

Cinderella is just one example of the sort of sub-textual messages often conveyed by traditional stories. Think about some of the others – Aladdin, Jack and the Beanstalk, Sleeping Beauty – and try a similar analysis of your own.

Traditional stories are part of our heritage, but it is important to be aware what the stories are saying beneath the surface, and to ensure that children are also exposed to other material which will offer alternative views.

Case Study - Stories

Lee was having a great time in the soft play area. With a group of friends he had built an elaborate obstacle course and was enjoying himself jumping and crawling through and balancing on a range of self-constructed challenges. The children shrieked with pleasure as they urged each other on. Suddenly the shrieks of delight were pierced by a scream. Lee had fallen from a piece of equipment and was howling loudly as he grasped one hand in the other. Hurrying to investigate, it soon became clear that as he had fallen Lee had landed on his hand and bent his finger back. The first-aider advised that Lee be taken to hospital to have his injured finger examined.

All the arrangements were made. Lee was to be taken to the hospital and his mother would meet them there. Although Lee had at first been upset he eventually calmed down and warmed to the idea of a trip out of school. Once on his way he was full of curiosity about everything around him. At the hospital he was eager to give first the receptionist, then the nurse and finally the doctor a full and frank account of what had happened.

The doctor explained that Lee would have to have an X-ray to find out whether his finger was broken. Lee wanted to know if he would be able to see the pictures. In X-ray he asked questions all the time and commented on every stage of the process. When his mother arrived, looking worried, she must have wondered what all the fuss was about. A beaming Lee greeted her with an enthusiastic invitation to view the pictures of his finger 'to see if it was broked!'.

When the X-ray was finally displayed Lee was fascinated. He could hardly believe that what he was looking at was 'inside his hand'. Fortunately nothing was broken, and all that was required was a sturdy bandage, which Lee wore with pride and pleasure. By this time, his mum was anxious to take him home but Lee was having none of it. He was determined to go back to school. Once there, Lee held the attention of ten adults and one hundred children, as he told the story of everything that had happened from beginning to end in great detail. As he did so he grew in self-confidence, visibly. Such is the power of story.

Case Study CONCLUSION

This example of a child's own **story telling** highlights the value of retelling experiences to an interested audience. The value to Lee in recounting his story, the value to the listening children in making sense of a frightening experience, and the value of support from parents, practitioners and professionals are all obvious. In addition, Lee's early development as an independent learner enabled him to ask questions and investigate a new and very interesting environment.

Quality CHECKLIST ✓

Ask yourself –

- Are children involved in decisions about which stories will be read and told?
- Do adults model the storytelling process?
- What are we doing to improve our own storytelling skills?
- How often do we 'act out' stories for the children?
- Do we support children in acting out their own stories?
- Do we talk about stories and how they are constructed?
- Are children encouraged to develop a critical response to the stories they hear?
- Do we accept children's storytelling contributions without judgement, allowing them to develop their expertise over time?
- Are children's own stories really valued by adults? How do we show that?
- Do we ever write down the stories children tell and read them back to them? Seeing their stories in writing helps children to realise the link between spoken and written language, and places a real value on what they have to say.
- Are children consulted about which new storybooks should be purchased?
- Do we help parents and carers to understand the value of story to children's development?

Resources for stories

Story telling is a different activity from story reading, and needs some different resources. Characters, objects, props, clothes and sound all help children to create and recreate stories. Of course, some of these will be influenced by the stories children hear – traditional tales, television settings, dreams and imaginings as well as real events in their lives. The practice children have in telling stories is a vital stage in preparing for story writing later in their education.

Creating stories can be fun. Try some of these resources

- Make up story boxes containing interesting things to stimulate storytelling – dinosaurs, space, under the sea, in the jungle, at the zoo, the seaside, and so on. Decorate the insides of the boxes for whatever themes or topics you have decided to cover.
- Make collections of artefacts. Try old maps, keys, binoculars, coins, etc.
- Have a listening corner where children can select and listen to story tapes.
- Provide a tape recorder so children can record their own stories.
- Have a wide range of puppets which children can use for story building.
- Use 'Flannelgraphs' to assist children in story making.
- Puppets and large dolls are readily available from educational catalogues, but are expensive. It's not difficult to make your own. Let the children help. The dolls will acquire personalities as the children talk about them.
- Boxes, baskets and containers are useful to create suspense and support prediction.
- Simple clothing – scarves, hats, capes and so on help create a character.
- Use perfumes, textures, flavours, sounds to excite all the senses during a story telling session.

ICT Box

- Use the computer to generate story boards for their own stories.
- Make video, slide or photo story books. These can either be shown on screen or printed off.
- Show children how to tape record their own stories. They could make 'listening books' for the group by taping and making a book of pictures.
- Use microphones to help children's confidence in speaking in a group. You could use one in circle time.
- Record sound effects tapes to go with stories.

We Can Do It!

Getting started with stories!

- **Send a letter** to the children from a fictional character or a soft toy character, creating a situation to which they can make a response. For example: Spot could be on his holidays and want the children to help him record his adventures upon his return; Mrs Wishy-Washy could have run out of soap; Kipper might like to have a birthday party; The Three Bears may be fed up with porridge and want information about alternative breakfasts.

- Collect half a dozen small objects at random. **Wrap them up in a parcel** and have it delivered to your room by someone else. The children can speculate on the contents and, once they have opened the parcel, who it has come from and why it has come to them.

- Make a collection of old **photographs and pictures** of interesting characters and encourage the children to make up stories around them.

- **Sit a large toy or doll on your knee.** Say to the children, "Charlie is very sad (or happy, or afraid, or tired) today. What do you think has happened to him?" Use questions to keep the children's stories developing.

- **Puppets** (or large dolls) are not difficult to use. Simply sit the puppet on a chair and let the story making begin. The moment you introduce them to the children you will find that they engage with them. They can make decisions about what the puppets should be called, where they live, who they live with and the things they like to do.

- **Create some open-ended story starters.** For example, disobeying the instructions of a parent or teacher (either consciously or unconsciously), going somewhere they have been told not to go, or taking something that does not belong to them. Begin the story and let the children carry it on.

- Invite **storytellers** into your setting

- Plan a story telling **event**.

Story starters ideas...

- Continue the story of the Three Bears or another familiar story. What happened next?
- Leave a bag or case of holiday items in the story corner.
- Take a sequence of photos of a story character puppet in your garden or another place.
- Collect some sound makers and use these as the stimuli for a story.
- Children love stories about you (when you were young or now!).
- Introduce a story about your pet or your own children.

Writing

> "Authors are people who make decisions; take responsibility for the selection of what goes on paper and are sensitive to ... contexts ... and audiences."
>
> Nigel Hall in 'Writing with Reason'

Introduction

QCA Guidance for the Foundation Stage suggests that we should be giving children opportunities to see adults speaking, listening, reading and writing. Children pick up their attitudes to learning from what they observe of adults, so we should be demonstrating for them in our daily behaviour the communication skills we want them to acquire. We should immerse them 'in an environment rich in print and possibilities for communication' encouraging them 'to recognise the importance of written language through signs, notices and books.'

The Guidance also advises that children should have chances to share and enjoy a wide range of stories, poems, rhymes and non-fiction books, to experiment with writing through mark making and to begin to understand how print works.

Links with Early Learning Goals

Goals associated with writing are found throughout the six areas. Here are some of the key ones:

Personal, Social & Emotional Development
- Continue to be interested, excited and motivated to learn.
- Be confident to try new activities, initiate ideas.

Language, Communication and Literacy
- Enjoy listening to and using spoken and written language, and readily turn to it in their play and learning.
- Explore and experiment with sounds, words and texts
- attempt writing for various purposes, using features of different forms such as lists, stories, instructions.
- Write their own names and labels and form sentences, sometimes using punctuation.
- Use their phonic knowledge to write simple regular words and make phonetically plausible attempts at more complex words.
- Use a pencil effectively and hold it effectively to form recognisable letters, most of which are correctly formed.

Physical Development
- Handle tools, with increasing control.

Creative Development
- Express and communicate their ideas, thoughts and feelings by using a widening range of materials.

Explanation/discussion

Mark making and writing offer good ways to promote independent learning. Even in this age of ICT, writing by hand is still important. Children who have access to high quality equipment and who are offered choice, freedom, support and recognition for their efforts will become writers. Just as children need free access to play materials and the outside environment, they need access to materials and equipment for mark making, an environment rich in print, and a place where they have models of adults and other children as writers. Learning about the purposes of writing is part of the process of becoming a writer, and the best way to learn this is to write and to see others writing and mark making. There should be frequent practice of writing activities in real life situations at home, within the setting, in the local community and in role play of all sorts.

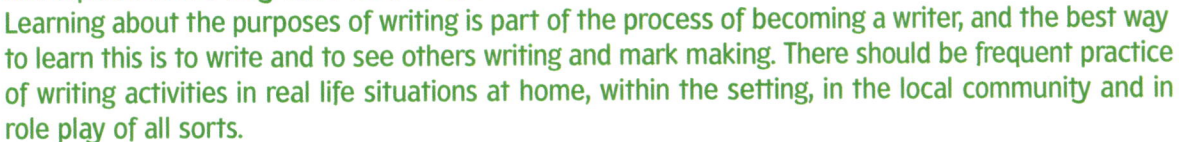

How children learn:

Children learn by doing. They learn to talk by talking, they learn to read by reading and they learn to write by writing. They eventually need to learn the orthodox way of forming letters and they need to realise that writing has meaning which can be interpreted by the reader, but in the earliest stages of writing children need the freedom to experiment.

Children need to...

EXPLORE! TRY-OUT! PRACTISE! ADAPT! EXPAND!

They need to compare the marks they make with the writing they see. As in all their learning, at first the process is much more important than the product. If the materials, models and equipment are available, children's first experiences of writing will usually be in role play or at writing tables, and will involve writing messages, labels, lists and letters. If every role play situation, inside and outside, offers materials for writing and mark making, they will be used. If every adult in the setting models writing as a useful and important activity - talking about what they are writing, reading back observations, explaining messages and letters, making lists with the children, writing recipes, transcribing the children's thoughts and descriptions of work to use as captions and labels - children will begin to make the link between what is spoken and what is written. If every visitor and every visit involves writing lists, notes and letters, and children's attention is drawn to writing in offices, shops, surgeries, fire-stations, garages, they will use these experiences in their own play. The aim is for children to begin to see the relationship between their own writing and the writing they see around them.

We Can Do It!

Case Study – Writing

David and Shahida are in the domestic role play area. David is dressed as the mum, Shahida is dressed as a nurse. She is visiting the house to see the new baby. In her nurse's bag she has a notebook, a pen and a mobile 'phone.

Shahida examines the baby. She looks carefully in the baby's ears, listens to his chest and gives him an 'injection'. David asks, "Is he OK?".

"Yes," says Shahida. "I'll give you a letter so you can show your husband." She gets out her notebook and writes a note. Then she folds it up and gives it to David, who offers her a cup of tea. As he puts the note in his pocket he says, "Your 'phone is ringing.".

Shahida answers the 'phone. "Just a minute," she says. "I need to write the address down." She writes some numbers and letters on her pad. "I can't have a cup of tea, I've got to get back to the hospital."

Shahida leaves the house. She crosses the room and stops at the writing table, leaning over to watch her friend Paddy, who is making a card for his grandma's birthday. He has chosen a piece of orange card and some feathers. He uses these to make the front of the card, saying as he works, "This is a flower for my Nan. This is the leaves, and this is the sun – there, its finished." He notices Shahida watching him. "Do you wanna make one? It's for my Nan. I'm gonna write inside when its dry."

Shahida shakes her head. She continues on her way across the room, meeting one of the adults and two children in aprons as she goes. "Do you want to come and make some biscuits with us?" they say. Shahida joins the cooking group. She helps to 'read' the pictorial recipe and to follow the steps it contains. When she has finished she returns to the writing table, draws a picture of the cooking session and writes the names of the children in the group above each head. She uses her emerging knowledge of phonics to identify the first letter of each name. Underneath the picture she writes her own name and the word 'Bscts'. She takes her picture to one of the adults, who reads it with her and helps her to pin it on the display board by the writing table.

Meanwhile, Paddy has returned to the writing corner to check on his card. It is dry, so he carefully opens it and inside he writes:
Grn Happy Brfdy
Love from Paddy
XXXXXX
He finds an envelope in the drawer and writes Grn on the outside. He puts the card into the envelope and takes it to his coat peg, where he balances it on top of his coat, "So I don't forget it".

Case Study — CONCLUSION

Writing is everywhere in this example of good practice with children moving easily from reading to writing and back again. They are gaining real experience of the purposes and the audiences for the messages they make. They are confident to attempt writing of letters and numbers, and can select the resources they need for this. The adults in the setting observe the children carefully and make sure that writing is modelled, valued and displayed, and that resources are accessible and inviting.

Quality CHECKLIST ✓

Ask yourself –

- Do we have a writing/mark making area in our setting? Are materials for writing and mark making also located where they are most likely to be used? Can children get at them easily?
- Are writing implements right for the ages and stages of development of the children? For example, are there different sizes of pencils, crayons and scissors for different sized hands? Do the scissors really cut, are pencils sharp? What do we provide to meet the various sorts of special needs?
- Is there enough of everything?
- Are the children encouraged to write as part of their play? Do we include writing in every role play situation? Are there opportunities to write outside?
- Is the writing and mark making equipment of the highest quality that the setting can afford? Do we always insist on the best for the children?
- Do we have a good range of equipment – for both boys and girls, to reflect diversity and the local community?
- Do we provide models of adults as writers? Do we explain and share the writing we do? What could we do to improve the models we offer?
- Do we exploit possibilities in stories, visits, visitors and the community to explore the reasons for writing?
- Do we promote 'emergent' writing and writers? Do we value process as well as product in writing?
- What is the balance in our setting between child initiated and adult directed writing?
- Are parents involved in helping children to understand the purposes of writing?

Resources for writing

Make the writing corner or table an area that is used every day. Involve the children in the choosing the contents, organisation and location. Also make sure the resources are interesting and easy to access. Change or add to the resources from time to time to sustain interest and give new ideas.

For writing activities, provide:

- Coloured paper, card, sticky labels, badges and several sizes of envelopes (recycled ones are fine, so tell your friends or the school office).
- A range of sizes, types and colours of pens, pencils, crayons (some children really like a fine pen for writing or drawing).
- Rulers, calculators, scissors, small staplers, glue sticks, stickytape.
- A letter writing table with a post box for children to send each other letters.
- Real life address books, diaries, appointment books (children are quite happy with used ones).
- Ready made books (two or three sheets of paper stapled together) for stories.
- Keyboards, computers with word processing sofware.
- Stamps (make your own by running a sewing machine – no cotton – across paper to make the perforations, then draw the pictures).
- Telephones, 'phone books, street maps, junk mail, forms, timetables, leaflets.

Some ideas for outside:

- Clip boards for game scoring.
- Playground chalk for directions and messages.
- Signs, notices and instructions (encourage the children to make their own notices).
- Spotter sheets for nature watching.
- A big blackboard screwed to the wall.

Model how to use a word processor by typing children's stories as they dictate them.

Use scanners or simple ClipArt to decorate covers or illustrate stories (be careful that children don't become reliant on ClipArt!).

Use the digital camera and/or video to capture real stories and events for children to talk and write about.

Explore touch screen software systems which allow children to draw direct onto the screen or on a special pad.

ICT Box

We Can Do It!

Getting started with writing!

- Put forms and junk mail in **home corners**.
- **'Plant' a letter** from a story book or local character in the room for the children to find.
- Write invitations and thank you letters to **visitors**.
- Scribe their **comments** to put with their pictures and models.
- Each time you put up a new caption, sign or notice, **read it** with the children.
- Make **lists** of things to do, what you need for a project or visit.
- **Explain** the writing you do – registers, notes to parents, messages and reminders, labels, planning, observations and read these to the children.
- Bring your **personal writing** to share with them - letters, cards, lists, instructions, diaries.
- **Encourage** the children and everyone you know to send you and the children postcards and letters.
- When you buy **new materials,** involve the children involved in what is needed, making lists and even doing the shopping.
- Offer to act as **scribe** for their stories (see the story section), captions, thoughts and comments.
- **Value their writing.** Put up a pin board at child height and encourage them to pin up their own writing. Encourage them to talk about their displays.
- Behave as though their emergent writing **means something** and you understand it. Encourage them to read their writing to you.
- Paint a cardboard box red and cut a slot in it. Tell the children it's a **post box** and they can use it to send letters to other children, adults in the settings, mums and dads. Clear it often and make sure all the letters are delivered. Write letters yourself to the children and encourage replies.
- When a child has made something, say **'I'd really like to know how you did that**. Can you write it down for me so that I can remember it?'.
- With the children, **collect examples** of different sorts of writing. Look at lists, forms, labels, instructions as well as stories, poems, diaries, letters – so they experience a wide range of purposes for writing. Help them to make their own collections.

Writing ideas for starters...

- A **café** or coffee shop with bills, menus and pads for the waiters and waitresses.
- A **doctor's surgery** with prescriptions.
- A **fire station** with a 'phone message pad.
- A **hairdresser's** with appointment cards and appointment book.
- An **office** with a computer (or just a keyboard), letters and envelopes.
- A **take away pizza place** with message pads, orders and trucks for delivery.

We Can Do It!

Systems, Structures & Organisation
to Promote Independent Learning

The aspects of the curriculum discussed so far in this book are concerned with specific activities and resources. This final section addresses some of the systems and structures within a Foundation Stage setting which facilitate and aid the sorts of learning experiences we have discussed and described. The systems must be adapted to suit the age and stage of development of individuals and groups, and the unique setting in which you work.

Helping children to organise themselves and take care of their personal belongings is a constant concern for practitioners, parents and the children themselves. Parents' anxiety is shown in the way they take over from them, doing things for them that, given a little time and space, children could do perfectly well for themselves – fetching coats, organising bags, looking for lost items of clothing, and so on. Children display anxiety by standing helplessly while adults organise them, by hanging on ferociously to tokens from home so they don't get lost, or by saying angrily, "I can do that, don't rush me!"

Suggestions

Here are some suggestions for helping children to organise themselves – and us:

- Check the height of door handles and the ease of opening of the doors. Children must be safe, but they shouldn't feel trapped.
- Make sure the pegs are at child height and far enough apart for children to manage. Space round a peg will improve access and tidiness, particularly for winter clothes. Bigger hooks make for ease of use. A shelf underneath serves as storage and a perch for changing shoes.
- Have a sewing session for parents and put a tape for hanging in each child's coat. Write the child's name on it before you sew it in.
- Label pegs and drawers with photographs of the children. A digital or Polaroid camera makes this easier to organise.
- Write names on large clothes pegs, shoes and wellies and use them to peg together.
- A simple cloth bag hanging on each peg will accommodate small belongings such as gloves and hats. Encourage the children to personalise them using fabric crayons
- A low shelf and some name labels will ensure safety for toys and other treasures brought from home.
- A box just inside the door is useful for jumpers and other clothes removed in the garden.

We Can Do It!

Support

Supporting children's developing sense of self-image and identity is another important area of early years work.

Here are some ideas:

- Set up self registration with **Velcro** cards, pockets or boxes. Have photographs as well as names to convey identity. Make some for staff as well.
- Photograph boards and books with pictures of each child, their family and friends are sources of endless interest. Add some photographs of children's homes, pets, and so on.
- Take the children out to take pictures of the community and local places of social and cultural interest.
- Children love sending and receiving messages and letters. Make some message boxes from shoe boxes, and provide a message writing table.
- Use names and/or photographs to identify individual cups and other personal articles.
- Involve the children in deciding the rules for play, what is fair and what is reasonable.
- The bathrooms and toilets should be well organised, pleasant places. Check towels, toilet paper and taps to ensure they are easy to use and in the right place. Mirrors, flowers and plants make a lot of difference, and a chair or stool helps the place to look more homely.

Planning and organising

Children can also be involved in planning and organising their own day and week. Of course, they need the opportunity to practise this and to realise that planning is a support, not a straitjacket.

In order to do this children need:

- uninterrupted time to engage in self chosen activities;
- support from adults as they plan and organise their activities;
- easy access to equipment and materials;
- stability in the routine of the day and the location of equipment;
- easy ways of recording what they are going to do, in pictures, symbols and charts;
- recognition and praise for taking responsibility for their own activities.

If needs are met, children can:
- decide what to do for at least part of the day;
- choose when (and where) to have snacks and drinks, and contribute to their organisation and content;
- think about tomorrow at the end of today;
- use charts, pictures with *Velcro* on the back, stickers or stamps to plan out their day;
- decide who to play with;
- make choices about joining group times;
- flow freely between indoors and the outdoors;
- help to plan trips, visits and outings;
- comment on the organisation of the setting;
- contribute to systems of rules, rewards and sanctions;
- have more input into when and how adult involvement would be helpful.

Setting Out and Clearing Up

Children can also be better involved in setting out and clearing up if they have more ownership of their activities. They see the importance of good organisation, they know where things are stored, they have an increased sense of responsibility for the equipment.

To do this, they could:
- help with the labelling and organisation of the room and the outside;
- make suggestions about combinations of different sorts of materials;
- contribute to choosing new equipment and resources by looking at catalogues and visiting shops;
- label and caption their own models, pictures, constructions;
- decide whether they want to dismantle a project or construction – whether they have 'finished with it';
- contribute to discussions about what went well and what worked;
- talk about what they learned and achieved during an activity;
- recognise the success of planning their own programme and the achievements of others;
- make their own 'record of achievement' and collections of work;
- take photographs, make labels and displays, give demonstrations, invite visitors, record their own commentaries, explanations, directions either alone or with the help of other children or adults.

Check your provision

When examining your systems and structures, the following checklist might be useful.

Are there:
- opportunities to work inside and out?
- opportunities to work alone and with others?

- areas for reflection and contemplation?
- places to write and read?
- places to leave work that is unfinished?
- tidy, well organised spaces for storing resources?
- opportunities to combine materials in new and creative ways?
- opportunities to extend and complement activities outside?
- places for display?
- Plants, pictures artefacts to interest them and do they reflect local cultures?
- child friendly furnishings and furniture?
- Finally, are resources accessible? At the right height? Visible? Well labelled? In cupboards or drawers that are easy to reach and open? Safe for children to use?

CONCLUSION

Have Fun!

Our original draft of this chapter offered readers an apology for its length. Now we are less inclined to make excuses! We feel that here is the kernel of what we are trying to achieve in this book. The philosophy, psychology and history of child development are very important. Case studies and accounts of practice elsewhere can provide useful ideas and pointers. But it is the actual, practical, day-to-day experiences of children in their settings which will enable and empower them as independent thinkers and set them on the way to becoming confident, competent and successful learners.

We hope you will find our advice useful, either by confirming the value of what you do already or suggesting some new ideas you could try. Or perhaps a little of both. Do, please, refer to **Foundations for Independence** for further help and guidance.

And good luck!

> "Being at the edge of what they can manage is where learning happens. It is when the environment that we set up for children enables them to be adventurous and show physical and social courage that children can begin to understand themselves and others."
>
> **Marjorie Ouvry in 'Exercising Muscles and Minds'**

> "Children need to feel safe enough to take risks, make mistakes and be adventurous."
>
> **QCA, Curriculum Guidance for the Foundation Stage**

> "A lack of independence to explore can seriously affect young children's learning and their development in many ways."
>
> **Jacqui Cousins in 'Listening to Four Year Olds'**

We Can Do It!

Further Reading

The core book from which We Can Do It has been developed is:

Featherstone, Sally & Bayley, Ros	Foundations for Independence	2001	Featherstone Education

Further Reading

Biddulph, Steve	Raising Boys	1998	Thorsons
Call, Nicola with Featherstone, Sally	The Thinking Child	2002	Network Press
Call, Nicola with Featherstone, Sally	The Thinking Child Resource Book	2003	Network Press
Cousins, Jacqui	Listening to Four Year Olds	1999	National Early Years Network
Curtis, Audrey	A Curriculum for the Pre-school Child	1960	NFER – Nelson
DfES/QCA	Curriculum Guidance for the Foundation Stage	2000	DfES
Duffy, Bernadette	Supporting Creativity and Imagination in the Early Years	1998	OUP
Goldschmeid, E & Jackson, S	People under Three	1994	Routledge
Goleman, Daniel	Emotional Intelligence	1995	Basic Books, New York
Greenman, Jim	Caring Spaces, Learning Places	1988	Exchange Press
Hall, Nigel (Ed)	Writing With Reason	1989	Hodder and Stoughton
Hannaford, Carla	Smart Moves	1995	Great Ocean
Hohman and Weikart	Educating Young Children	1995	High/Scope Press
Katz (Ed)	Reflections on the Reggio Emilia	1994	University of Illinois
Lindon, Jennie	Too Safe for their own Good?	1999	National Early Years Network
Miller, Judy	Never too Young : How children can take responsibility and make decisions	1996	National Early Years Network
Nutbrown, Cathy	Threads of Thinking	1999	Paul Chapman
Ouvry, Marjorie	Exercising Muscles & Minds	2000	National Early Years Network
Reggio Children	The Hundred Languages of Children		Reggio Children
Weisman Topal, Cathy & Gandini, Lella	Beautiful Stuff	1999	Davis
Lewisham (LEARN)	A Place to Learn 2002, available from eys.advisers@lewisham.gov.uk		

Useful Websites

Featherstone Education	www.featherstone.uk.com
High/Scope Initiative	www.highscope.org
Sure Start Initiative	www.surestart.gov.uk